See You Later Alligator

Veloisa Diana Simpson

Published and Distributed by:
Professional Publishing House
1425 W. Manchester Ave., Suite B
Los Angeles, California 90047
www.professionalpublishinghouse.com
email: professionalpublishinghouse@yahoo.com
(323) 750-3592

First printing: October 2018
ISBN: 978-0-9983089-8-2
10987654321

See You Later Alligator

Part I

See You Later Alligator

A Friend

Personal

Social

Professional

See You Later Alligator

A Friend

A Friend is Compassionate,

Sympathetic, Humble.

See You Later Alligator

Smile!

VELOISA DIANA SIMPSON

See You Later Alligator

A Friend

A friend is someone who

loves you

no matter what you have done.

See You Later Alligator

Smile!

See You Later Alligator

A friend cries when you

Are saddened

And laughs when you

Need to have fun.

See You Later Alligator

Smile!

See You Later Alligator

A Friend

A friend walks with you on the path of life, and

Together you share,

The beauty the strength

The wonder of the Ones

That dwells everywhere!

See You Later Alligator

Smile!

See You Later Alligator

A Friend

God loves us, and a friend

tells us so.

See You Later Alligator

Smile!

See You Later Alligator
A Friend

A friend is a priceless

Gem for the crown of

Life here and cherish a

Star in memory forever.

See You Later Alligator

Smile!

See You Later Alligator
A Friend

My friends are little

Lamps to me.

When I lose a friend,

A little lamp goes out.

VELOISA DIANA SIMPSON

See You Later Alligator

Smile!

21

See You Later Alligator

A Friend

A friend who is far away

is still there to think of, to

wonder about, to hear from,

to write, to share life and

experiences with, to serve, to

honor, to admires, and to love.

See You Later Alligator

Smile!

See You Later Alligator

A Friend

There is no friend

Like the old friends

Who has shared our

Days, months and years.

See You Later Alligator

Smile!

See You Later Alligator

A Friend

What is it to stay

young?

It is the ability to hold

fast to old friends and to

make new ones, to open

our hearts quickly to a light

that knocks on the door.

VELOISA DIANA SIMPSON

See You Later Alligator

Smile!

27

See You Later Alligator
A Friend

Friends are the

flowers in the

garden of life.

See You Later Alligator

Smile!

See You Later Alligator

After Awhile

Crocodile

VELOISA DIANA SIMPSON

See You Later Alligator

A Friend

Keep Smiling

31

Part II

See You Later Alligator

Being Your Own

Best Friend

Valoisa Diana Simpson

See You Later Alligator

To those who

have become their

Own Best Friend.

See You Later Alligator
Being Your Own
Best Friend

Smile!

See You Later Alligator
Being Your Own
Best Friend

It's important to learn to listen to ourselves.

If we learn to listen, we will find out a lot and we will hear some

wonderful things.

See You Later Alligator

Being Your Own

Best Friend

Smile!

See You Later Alligator
Being Your Own
Best Friend

You must learn to talk

to yourself. That's very

important. You need to explain things, to reassure

yourself. You need to

establish an ongoing

dialogue. It can help you

in many situations.

See You Later Alligator
Being Your Own
Best Friend

Smile!

See You Later Alligator
Being Your Own
Best Friend

If you pay attention,

You can take a

Moment and consider

What you really want to do

You have the power to

Stop yourself: this is a

Good thing to know. At

First it's hard, but it

Gets easier.

See You Later Alligator
Being Your Own
Best Friend

Smile!

See You Later Alligator
Being Your Own
Best Friend

There are no limits

To how much we can

grow and develop, but

time limits us.

People are often obsessed

With aging, and with

what time does to them. Instead

they should be concerned

about what they do

with time.

See You Later Alligator
Being Your Own
Best Friend

Smile!

See You Later Alligator

Being Your Own

Best Friend

If we learn to love

and nurture ourselves,

we would be richer than we could ever

imagine.

See You Later Alligator
Being Your Own
Best Friend

Smile!

See You Later Alligator

Being Your Own

Best Friend

We are all accustomed

to someone giving

us a kind word, but

we really have available

to ourselves many

kind words.

See You Later Alligator
Being Your Own
Best Friend

Smile!

See You Later Alligator
Being Your Own
Best Friend

We can help ourselves to change,

to grow, to become the person we were created to be.

It is in us to be our own

Best Friend

www.ingramcontent.com/pod-product-compliance
Lightning Source LLC
Chambersburg PA
CBHW070830100426
42813CB00003B/557